# THE BIG BOOK
# OF EXIT
# STRATEGIES

ne likes lists
lots of voltas

# THE BIG BOOK OF EXIT STRATEGIES

## JAMAAL MAY

ALICE JAMES BOOKS
FARMINGTON, MAINE

10 9 8 7 6 5 4 3 2 1

Alice James Books are published by Alice James Poetry Cooperative, Inc.,
an affiliate of the University of Maine at Farmington.

Alice James Books
114 Prescott Street
Farmington, ME 04938
www.alicejamesbooks.org

Library of Congress Cataloging-in-Publication Data

Names: May, Jamaal, author.
Title: The big book of exit strategies / Jamaal May.
Description: Farmington, ME : Alice James Books, [2016]
Identifiers: LCCN 2015036403 | ISBN 9781938584244
(softcover : acid-free paper)
Subjects: | BISAC: POETRY / American / African American.
Classification: LCC PS3613.A948 A6 2016 | DDC 811/.6--dc23
LC record available at http://lccn.loc.gov/2015036403

Alice James Books gratefully acknowledges support from individual donors,
private foundations, the University of Maine at Farmington, and the National
Endowment for the Arts.

**ART WORKS.**
arts.gov

Contributions for the production of The Big Book of Exit Strategies made by:
David & Gail Levine, Judith Michaels, and Gerard Mitchell.

Cover Art: "The Cycle" by Brian Despain

# Contents

———— ⚜ ————

———————— ⚓ ————————

# Acknowledgments

I'm grateful to the periodicals and anthologies in which earlier versions of the following poems first appeared:

*The Believer*, "Conducting Ivy with the Girl Down the Street"
*Best American Poetry 2015* (Simon & Shuster), "There Are Birds Here"
*The Book of Scented Things* (Literary House Press), "Per Fumum"
*Callaloo*, "Intake in the Ward," "Megalophobia," "It Shakes Us Still"
*The Chattahoochee Review*, "Exit Interview," "For Years You Trained
    for Being Lost at Sea"
*The Cortland Review*, section from "A Brief History of Hostility" as
    "Pyrophobia"
*Crazyhorse*, "Against Against," "The Spirit Names of Stolen Books"
*Fogged Clarity*, "Make Believe," "Little Design"
*Indiana Review*, "The Gun Joke"
*Liberation* (Beacon Press), "FBI Questioning During the 2009
    Presidential Inauguration"
*Lumina*, "Petrified at The End of All Things," "Dare"
*The MacGuffin*, section from "A Brief History of Hostility" as "They
    May Come to Break Us"
*The Mainstreet Rag*, "Behind the Ward"
*New Republic*, "Ruin"
*Ninth Letter*, "From The Big Book of Exit Strategies," "Sugar,"
    "History as Road Trip from Detroit to Mississipi"

*PEN.org*, "Ode To the White-Line-Swallowing Horizon," "God of the Ocean of Lumber," "Open Mouth Requiem," "Ode to Forgetting"

*Ploughshares*, "Things That Break"

*Poem* (UK), "FBI Questioning During the 2009 Presidential Inauguration," "This is How I Know it Might Work"

*Poem a Day*, "I Have This Way of Being"

*Poetry*, "There Are Birds Here," "Per Fumum," "Water Devil," "Respiration"

*PoetryNow*, "Shift"

*See Spot Run*, "Ask Where I've Been," "Mouth," "In the Future You Will Be Your Own Therapist";

*Sou'wester,* "The Whetting of Teeth"

*Water Stone*, "The Tendencies of Walls"

Thank you to organizations that supported the editing of this collection: The Lannan Foundation, *The Kenyon Review*, the Civitella Ranieri Foundation, and all the colleges, universities, high schools and community groups that graciously invited me to share, learn, and grow through my visits with them.

Of course, I am especially thankful for the emotional support and the skilled mind of amar priyo kobi, amar priyo kobita, Tarfia Faizullah.

*For us and them and them and us.*

# Ask Where I've Been

Let fingers roam
the busy angles
of my shoulders.
Ask why skin dries
in rime-white patches, cracks  *odd image*
like a puddle stepped on. Ask
about the scars that interrupt
blacktop, a keloid on my bicep:
this fogged window. Ask how many
days passed before the eyebrow healed
after a metal spike was torn out,
uprooted lamppost in a tornado.
Ask about the tornado of fists.
The blows landed. If you can
watch it all—the spit and blood frozen
against snow, you can probably tell
I am the too-narrow road winding out
of a crooked city built of laughter,
abandon, feathers, and drums.
Ask only if you can watch streetlights bow,
bridges arc, and power lines sag,
and still believe what matters most
is not where I bend
but where I am growing. *→ not "going"  I like*

1

# There Are Birds Here
## *For Detroit*

There are birds here,
so many birds here,
is what I was trying to say
when they said those birds were metaphors
for what is trapped
between fences
and buildings. No.

The birds are here
to root around for bread
the girl's hands tear
and toss like confetti. No,

I don't mean the bread is torn like cotton,
I said confetti, and no
not the confetti
a tank can make out of a building.
I mean the confetti
a boy can't stop smiling about,
and no his smile isn't much
like a skeleton at all. And no
their neighborhood is not like
a war zone.

I am trying to say
the neighborhood is as tattered
and feathered as anything else,
as shadow pierced by sun
and light parted
by shadow-dance as anything else,
but they won't stop saying

how lovely the ruins,
how ruined the lovely
children must be
in your birdless city.

# Ode to the White-Line-Swallowing-Horizon

Apologies to the moths that died in service
to my windshield's cross-country journey.  *lol*
Apologies to the fine country cooking
vomited into a rest stop bathroom.
Apologies to the rest stop janitor.
To the mop, galvanized bucket,
sawdust, and push broom—the felled
tree it was cut from, dulled saw, blistered hand,

I offer my apologies. To the road.
To the white-line-swallowing-horizon.
I've used you almost up.

I'm sorry I don't know another way
to push the charcoal outline of that house
into the ocean-dark behind me.
For being a grown man
with a boogeyman at his back.

Apologies to the grown man growing out
of a splintering boy's body, all apologies due
to the splinters. Little ones,
you should've been a part of something whole.

*I- not sure I understand this it got too broad*

4

# Things That Break

Skin of a plum. Rotting tooth.

Switches cut down by a child
to lash a child's legs.

A siege does something like this
against sturdy walls. The wrong rules. *not just rules*

A dozen angel figurines flying
from a balcony.

Flailing fist. Splint.
Forefinger and index,

dislocated (not broken). One points
to the left of a man

and the rubbery thing inside quivers

familiar. Raise your hand
if you know how to do this.

If enough hair fails to escape
the pull of a drain, and the drain

5

sputters and fails to swallow water,
we will likely say it's broken.

Waves. Traffic lights.

The craven infantry
of roaches at the flick of a switch.

Will—a child in a shrinking living room
sitting more still than the father.

# As the Saying Goes *not quite! :)*

A bird in the hand
smells like a human.
A closed mouth gathers
a storm of questions.
A coward dies. A
hero dies. A civilian dies—
thousands of deaths.

A fool and his money
are soon pardoned.
Children should be seen
as a herd of elephant feet.
If you can't beat them,
beat them. Cold steel,
warm slug. No guts,
no voice, no bones. No news is good.
Nothing ventured, nothing stained
burgundy. A gurney of a thousand screams
begins with a single death.

A thorn is a thorn is a thorn.
Absence makes the heart grow maggots.
All roads lead to gravestone.
Not all that glitters fits into a jar.

All's well that ends.
April showers the graveyard
with apple blossom petals.
Any storm in a drought.
Ask not what my country will do to you…
Ashes and ashes and dust and dust and
dust and ashes and dust.

# FBI Questioning During the 2009 Presidential Inauguration

*Have you always been named Jamaal?*

Yes, my name means beauty.
Yes, my name is Gemal in Egypt
and Cemal in Turkey. In Kosovo
Xhemal, and Dzemal in Bosnia.
What it means, in the language
you fear, is beauty has always lived
with the sound of *awe* at its center.

*How long have you lived in Detroit?*

Ivy leaves have taken back
a house on the block
where the memory of me is still climbing
the slope of a leveled garage.
A yellow excavator has taken one in its mouth.
The temptation to become ash
has claimed several others.

*Are there any explosives in the house?*

The new president's hand
presses to a bible like a branding iron,
and I want to say something
about the eruption of love poems
written by fifth graders on my shelf.
Which list carries my name?
I don't ask. How many Jamaals
are being questioned right now? I wonder,
but don't ask. The agents have not come
to burn the pages or cut out my tongue.
They are here to arrest the delusion
of a moment when anybody had one.

*Have you spent much time overseas?*

I tried to paint an ocean
across my bedroom wall,
but my blood reddened
as soon as it hit air.

I wanted to build a house
from my name, but every letter
in every word was as thin as my arms.

It would be nice to quarantine the county,
tape off city blocks, make a fence
of my teeth, and protect every laugh
inside the borders of me, but when I reach…

the hurried unravel of sinew,
that peculiar popping sound in my ankle.
Teach me how to get my hands
into the air without the gods
knowing about it, because I hear static
sometimes, wonder if my voice is being taped—
listen, listen; someone is writing us down.

# Conducting Ivy with the Girl Down the Street

The way the house says

*spider web*

in a voice

that looks like aerial roots

scaling the face
the way her free hand

and mine swoop

and lift air

like they belong

to conductors

the way our batons pretend

to not be gnarled sticks

the way crescendo smells

like ivy leaves and brick—

it's almost as if we know what we're doing.

Every flourish

conjures more flora

to reclaim

the crossbeams and silica.

When I say        *flutes*

                              and swing my stick

                     like a machete

                              through waist-high grass


she tells me what the swish of it looks like.


I try to picture a sliver

                              of wind

detect the sound's arc.

It's there for a moment

                              then lost in the shadow

of the building

                              our orchestra of vine and leaf

hasn't quite devoured whole.

When I say        *strings*

                              the girl sings

                              without notes

or words          eyes closed

head lolling

          like the breeze

                     is doing something

electric to her hair.

She describes the shade of blue gusting

          out of her baton

                              as it moves

like an archet

over strings.
And when she says          *drums*
I break
          into a broken
                    little beatbox
but she covers my mouth
kisses the back of her hand
                    and begins
to articulate
          the green
          that just keeps rising out of us.

# From The Big Book of Exit Strategies

Fig 5: Sunlight hits a grate on its way to her
legs where it casts fishnet stockings
of shadow, or a crosshatch cage for the bees
tattooed on each leg just above the knees.

Fig 12: This is where the American's bullet
went in, he mumbles into his hoisted shirt.
Not pictured: exit wound.

Fig 58: The terrain here is hungry
for the roots of trees and whatever else
it can find: fruit fallen from limbs, flesh
and fur, organs and cartilage. They belong
trapped in the earth until the waves come.
The waves always come.

Fig 5: He slides a hand under the grate-shadow
to imprison the roads on his palm,
thinking of a map in a glove box, all roads
that never led to anything remembered as sweet.

Fig 43: The shriek of a vesper bat tells it
everything it needs to know about this mason jar
holding leather wings to its face. Not pictured:
the hand that will fling it at a tree.

Figure 2: Their hands are small theaters
where bodies come to laugh and come to
come alive like the space between steel
and flint. Belly of flint, stomach of steel—
they learn to pronounce *conflagration*
from this position.

Fig 21: A woman caught in a snarl of bushes
finds her skin grated by branch
less in the initial collision, more
in the clumsy extraction of limbs
from what obviously doesn't want her
but will claw to keep her.

Fig 13: This is where the bullet came out.
Not pictured: entry wound.

Fig. 57: A fisherman pulls his nets from the waters
and finds a version of himself twisted in them,
gasping for air that is all around him
but inaccessible because some god
put gills where there should have been lungs,

and his skin, which should have been skin,
is a flex of scale that will be useless
if he ever does make it ashore.

Fig 7: He flinches when she releases
the clasp of his belt.

Fig 9: She is the forgotten child
on the snowy stoop still. After all the snow
that will cover her has covered her
and someone has come to find her shiver,
she will be the door closing in her face,
the flurries gathering about the shoulders.

Fig 5: Here, the caption says *honeybees,*
but the tattoos are of wasps.
Not pictured: the thousand kisses
they attract to their stingers and wings.

Fig 52: The ocean has a star in its mouth
or it's just that sunset shows a body
of water has teeth, gallons of teeth. Up to
three thousand in one shark alone
and the biggest star around these parts
goes down without any fight.

Fig 26: *I'm going down, don't let me die*,
a man screams his neighbors awake
after falling through pond ice. His clawing
for the cracking edges hastens the pull of water,
water so cold he can't feel it anymore.

Fig 14: His friend presses an amazed thumb
against the scar that glistens
dull like a frozen lake she's never seen.
Like the filthy glass sand becomes.
She touches its twin on the other side
and imagines that moment, when together,
they were the last wound opened and the next.

# The Gun Joke

It's funny, she says,
how many people are shocked by this shooting
and the next and next and the next.

She doesn't mean funny as in funny, but funny
as in blood soup tastes funny when you stir in soil.
Stop me if you haven't heard this one.

A young man/old man/teenage boy
walks into an office/nightclub/day care/church
and empties a magazine into a crowd of strangers/
enemies/family/students.

Ever hear the one about the shotgun? What do you call it
when a shotgun tests a liquor store's bulletproof glass?
What's the difference between a teenager
with hands in the air and a paper target charging at a cop?
What do you call it when a man sets his own house on fire,
takes up a sniper position, and waits for firefighters?
Stop me if you haven't heard this one before.

The first man to pull a gun on me
said it was only a joke,
but never so much as smiled.

The second said, *This is definitely not a joke*,
and then his laughter crackled through me
like electrostatic—funny how that works.

When she says it's funny she means funny
as in crazy and crazy as in
this shouldn't happen. This shouldn't happen
as in something is off. Funny as in
off—as in,
ever since a small caliber bullet chipped his spine,
your small friend walks kinda' funny
and his smile is off.

# Hoplophobia
*Fear of firearms*

*The most common manifestation of hoplophobia*
*is the idea that instruments possess a will of their own*
*apart from that of their user.*

—Lt. Colonel Jeff Cooper

A skinny kid came home last week
with the eyes of a man
and a perforated eardrum—
to think, someone used to know him.

He's memorized the laughter of small arms
fire, the mutterings of tank tread, and now
begs us to listen as he translates
this language of weaponry.
It's irrational, I'm sure,
but I can't help but remember
how a pocket knife once whispered open
and snarled at my mother's belly,
so I ask him to say more.

We talk about "Machine Gun"
by Hendrix until the flame flickers
back into his pupils and he's lost again,
cataloging the distinct dialect of munitions

chattering overhead—wrought iron coughs
and the smoke of a furnace pours
out of the invasion
that still surrounds him. Happens all the time.

Even survivors he found writhing
at the burnt remains of a marketplace
say they heard the bombs
long before they hit, screaming—
yes, screaming—in Arabic.

# A Brief History of Hostility

In the beginning
there was the war.

The war said let there be war
and there was war.

The war said let there be peace
and there was war.

The people said music and rain
evaporating against fire in the brush
was a kind of music
and so was the beast.

The beast that roared
or bleated when brought down
was silent when skinned
but loud after the skin
was pulled taut over wood
and the people said music
and the thump thump
thump said drum.
Someone said
war drum. The drum said war

is coming to meet you in the field.
The field said war
tastes like copper,
said give us some more, said look
at the wild flowers our war plants
in a grove and grows
just for us.

Outside sheets are pulling
this way and that.

Fields are smoke,
smoke is air.

We wait for fingers to be bent
knuckle to knuckle,

the porch overrun
with rope and shotgun

but the hounds don't show.
We beat the drum and sing

like there's nothing outside
but rust-colored clay and fields

of wild flowers growing
farther than we can walk.

Torches may come like fox paws
to steal away what we plant,

but with our bodies bound
by the skin, my arc to his curve,

we are stalks that will bend
and bend and bend…

fire for heat
fire for light
fire for casting figures on a dungeon wall

fire for teaching shadows to writhe
fire for keeping beasts at bay
fire to give them back to the earth

fire for the siege
fire to singe
fire to roast
fire to fuse rubber soles to collapsed crossbeams
fire for Gehenna

fire for Dante
fire for Fallujah
fire for readied aim

fire in the forge that folds steel like a flag
fire to curl worms like cigarette ash
fire to give them back to the earth

fire for ancient reasons: to call down rain
fire to catch it and turn it into steam
fire for churches
fire for a stockpile of books
fire for a bible-black cloak tied to a stake

fire for smoke signals
fire to shape gun muzzle and magazine
fire to leap from the gut of a furnace
fire for Hephaestus
fire for pyres' sake
fire licking the toes of a quiet brown man
fire for his home
fire for her flag
fire for this sand, to coax it into glass

fire to cure mirrors
fire to cure leeches
Fire to compose a nocturne of cinders

fire for the trash cans illuminating streets
fire for fuel
fire for fields
fire for the field hand's fourth death

fire to make a cross visible for several yards
fire from the dragon's mouth
fire for smoking out tangos
fire to stoke like rage and fill the sky with human remains
fire to give them back to the earth
fire to make twine fall from bound wrists
fire to mark them all and bubble black
any flesh it touches as it frees

They took the light from our eyes. Possessive.
Took the moisture from our throats. My arms,
my lips, my sternum, sucked dry, and
lovers of autumn say, *Look, here is beauty*.
Tallness only made me an obvious target made of
off-kilter limbs. I'd fall either way. I should get a
*to-the-death* tattoo or metal ribbon of some sort.
War took our prayers like nothing else can,
left us dumber than remote drones. Make
me a loyal soldier and I'll make you a
lamenting so thick, metallic, so tank-tread-hard.

Now make tomorrow a gate shaped like a man.
I can't promise, when it's time, I won't hesitate,
cannot say I won't forget to return in fall and
guess the names of the leaves before they change.

The war said bring us your dead
and we died. The people said music
and bending flower, so we sang ballads

in the aisles of churches and fruit markets.
The requiem was everywhere: a comet's tail
disappearing in the atmosphere,

the wide mouths of the bereft men that have sung…
On currents of air, seeds were carried
as the processional carried us

through the streets of a forgetting city,
between the cold iron of gates.
The field said soil is rich wherever we fall.

Aren't graveyards and battlefields
our most efficient gardens?
Journeys begin there too if the flowers are taken

into account, and shouldn't we always
take the flowers into account? Bring them to us.
We'll come back to you. Peace will come to you

as a rosewood-colored road paver
in your grandmother's town, as a trench
scraped into canvas, as a violin bow, a shovel,

an easel, a brushstroke that covers
burial mounds in grass. And love, you say,
is a constant blade, a trowel that plants

and uproots, and tomorrow
will be a tornado, you say. Then war,
a sick wind, will come to part the air,

straighten your suit,
and place fresh flowers
on all our muddy graves.

# The Unseen Hand of Zombie Jesus

Zombie Jesus looks a lot like the other guy,
but there are key differences.
Like the lack of scabs on his palms. His hands
are gone altogether, having rotted and fallen off
on a trek to Detroit's southwest side.
Zombie Jesus is said to have *healing nubs.*
Pilgrims claim that to merely touch the tattered hem
of his size small tunic is enough to restore
any fingers he may have chomped off
while you were praying. For Zombie Jesus,
water doesn't flow from barrels as a pinot noir,
but rest a sack of oregano near him and watch the magic—
Zombie Jesus knows how to uplift the people.
He doesn't require you to kneel—
his only commandment:
Get. Down.
So he throws fish fries and barbecues, inviting saints
and sinners alike. The man who is more
than a man can really hook up a steak, telekinetically
stoking Gehenna-hot flames and yelling,
*Look! No Hands.*

If he did have hands, they'd be calloused
but not bloodied because Zombie Jesus

wasn't crucified like the other guy.
He was pierced by a nail gun in the temple
of his skull. He was buried in a friend's grave
on top of that friend. There was no stone to roll away,
but he did have to punch through the coffin
and stagger on decomposing legs from a cemetery
to a city that wanted him dead.

The email account, *zombiejs2@me.com*,
reaches capacity daily with
*Improve your performance*,
*Make $$ from home,*
*Have you heard the good news?*
and a screech of prayers that will continue
to go unanswered, at least until
the injunction filed against him is cleared up;
that shit that went down in Rome:
totally not his fault.

Then, with the wave of a hand
that isn't even there, ZJC will draw mercury
from the fish, draw cancer
from some bone, water the Gobi, water
the lawn, walk your dog, take out the trash,
and open up the graves collapsed around
all of your trapped, twitching dead.

# Open Mouth Requiem

In the open mouths of our many graves
are the teeth of our many friends, mouths
open with the endless smiling
only skeletons can endure.

The dead find everything funny.
The living find everything dying
to be more alive than a phonograph
amplifier dropped into a bathtub.

A saying I can't forget goes something like:

tied to a chair, sent up in flames, the rope
was destroyed before the fire
convincingly claimed your cousin
belonged in its careful arms.

As the saying goes:

third degree burns across ninety percent
of his cringing skin
could not claim his voice
before a neighbor had endured its muttering,

having found him and eased him into a bathtub,
unsure of what one does with a dead man
who has yet to get around to dying.

Again, someone whispers something awful
into the ear of a co-worker, and another morning
haunts a lover with a sibling's empty voice,
*What if we just keep the box closed?*

Many mouths open and close
around so many children with tiny fists
for eyes, no one can stop remembering

how greedy the land is. How it calls
all of us back, spoiled by the ease
at which we always come.

# Petrified at the End of All Things

Having not been built to hold the slabs
of slate our handfuls of flowers become,
we must nevertheless carry them
into hospital rooms where those who promised
to be always un-endable
have become part plastic tubing,
part immodest gown and IV-thin voice.
Part leaving. Part staying.

Those who promised us streamers
and ridiculous hats for all time
keep calling us to their bedsides,
and we are smitten with the way they love
the end of all things, curling up next to it
like the end of all things
is a fur-covered creature
that can be coddled into reason.

But reason becomes a petrified branch
that splinters in a forest of undulating limbs.

37

# Yes, I Know She's Dying

Yes, I added a line about my dying friend
to paint myself sympathetically,
but also because it's all I think about now.
I warn you, this will dissolve
most of your good sense
for art too. I've been pacing my home, hell,
my entire city, waiting for a canvas
of anything to scream,
*Break me or let me break.*

I mouth her name to a god
whose language I don't speak.
I make metaphor for the empty
she is becoming — a trench opening
from the outside in, the inside of a fist,
decay-dark socket in the head
of a bleached cow skull —

because it's the only way
to make real the unreal
way she's disappearing
while showing up everywhere
and losing weight
while getting too heavy
for me to carry
and carry on the way I do.

# Mouth

Yours is no longer good for tearing flesh from flesh
or cartilage since they wired it shut because you couldn't
keep it closed after a sucker punch broke it open because
you couldn't keep it closed. But you mumble
about liking the soup, ramen noodles without the noodles,
the sound jello makes when it sluices between teeth and metal.

Mine is becoming a trap for what I don't say. What is bitter
choked down but no sweeter spit up, all copper
and slime, chipped from a rotted tooth, is spit,
blood, blood and spit. I'm afraid speaking will splinter
into a confession of how I like the muffled sea
of your voice, your jaw stilled by rigging.

# Love Poem Moving Back and Forth Across Glass
*For Tarfia*

One can't know how much
a construction barrel weighs
until it collides with a sleepy car

and snatches off the rearview mirror. Ok,
so now I know. The light
fixture said little more than *wind*

after it broke off the barrel,
scattered my window,
and landed in the passenger seat.

I watched it roll back and forth across
all that shifting glass for too long
before I stopped the car.

Instead of replacing the mirror,
I've since learned to move forward
without seeing a third of what's behind me.

I'm sorry sweet-love,
but I've missed you exactly
this way. When did we become fluid

in ghost-talk; poltergeists in the rooms of each other,
slamming doors and rattling cutlery
with our absence?

My haunted and haunting woman/my careening
kiss/sugared poison/my neuron on fire,
my longing for you is a hand

that pulled the shaken car
toward median, tossed a light
into a field, and collected hardly any cuts

brushing glass from empty seat to roadside.
My longing is my exhausted spine
gone slack against the autumn-cool car hood

as I wondered why that scattershot of stars
wasn't visible on the horizon as I drove, and yes,
it is the rest of that drive,

with its broken-window-gale-song.
Yes, my longing for you is a reminder
I didn't get all the shards

when headlights made them glitter
like the millions of distant sparks
that disappeared again as I drove,

checking back for a reflection
that wasn't there, the empty black
I couldn't see gather behind me

as I rattled forward, afraid
every direction I move has always been,
will one day be,

once was, and always is
toward the precarious cliff
of your collarbone.

# Make Believe

Tell me you are a lord
of jagged stones that were pillars.

Tell me I am wrong
about my skin, that it is no fortress.

What work of fiction can pacify
you who must sleepwalk the line
between what is real
and what is etch-a-sketch to survive?

Pretend the grass is deadly and press me deep
down in that forest of switchblades.

Pretend cement is lava hungry
to suck meat from your shins but I

am safe and solid. Can resist. Can't be
burned down or swallowed up. Pretend
the water is poison
and I will pretend to be poison.

# Per Fumum
## *Through Smoke*

My mom became an ornithologist
the moment a grackle tumbled
through barbecue smoke
and fell at her feet. Later

she explained why singers cage birds;
it can take weeks for them to memorize
just one wayward melody,
since the first days are a wash, lost
as they mope and warble the friendless tone
every animal memorizes hours into breathing.
It's the knell a bottle of cologne would sound
if it were struck while something arcane
was aligned with a planet that was even more mythic
but farther away. My dad was an astronomer
for twenty minutes in a row
the first time a bus took us so far away
from streetlights he could see clearly,
point out constellations
that may or may not have been Draco,
Orion, Aquila, or Crux. When they faded
I resented the sun's excess,
a combination of fires I couldn't even smell.

He told me the first chemist was a star perfumer.
Her combination for dizzy was brushed
against pulse points
so they could unlock when kissed
by quickening blood. From stolen perfumes
I concocted a toxin I could call my own
but learned it was no more deadly
than that same amount of water
to any creature the size of a roach.
I grew suspicious of my plate and lighter
Bunsen burner, the tiny vials accumulating
in my closet. I was a chemist for months
before I learned the difference
between poisoned and drowned.
When my bed caught fire
it smelled like a garden.

# I Have This Way of Being

I have this, and this isn't a mouth
      full of the names of odd flowers

I've grown in secret.
      I know none of these by name

but have this garden now,
      and pastel somethings bloom

near the others and others.
      I have this trowel, these overalls,

this ridiculous hat now.
      This isn't a lung full of air.

Not a fist full of weeds that rise
      yellow then white then windswept.

This is little more than a way
      to kneel and fill gloves with sweat,

so that the trowel in my hand
      will have something to push against,

rather, something to push
        against that it knows will bend

and give and return as sprout
        and petal and sepal and bloom.

# Respiration

A lot of it lives in the trachea, you know.
But not so much that you won't need more muscle:

the diaphragm, a fist clenching
but never landing a blow.

Inhale.

So many of us are breathless,
you know, like me

kneeling to collect the shards of a houseplant
my elbow has nudged into oblivion.

What if I sigh, and the black earth
beneath me scatters like insects

in the wake of that first breath?
Am I a god then? Am I insane

because I worry about ant colonies
and the disassembling of earth regularly?

I walk more softly now
into gardens or up the steps of old houses

with impatiens stuffing window boxes.
When it's you standing there with a letter

or voice or face full of ruined news, tell me,
will you hold your breath before you knock?

# Ruin

Ruin means the barn is on fire
or the house is in flames
or the soil is as fertile
as ash

or the belly swells with unwanted
limbs and yet another belly
to fill with this week's
wages.

Ruination means the barn is full
of livestock when it collapses
and the fertile are ash
in soil

or the unwanted swell in numbers
until the shelter is fat
like the belly
of a hog.

Fire means clean in the way
clean means erasure
in that peculiar
way erasure

means an ugly kind of dead, the face
a scorched topography, ruined
into an unrecognizable
relief.

# The Tendencies of Walls

My nostalgia is a pyromaniac
I follow into a condemned barn
that once served as a nightclub

as if there were a dance
left in any of us.
As if we'd find ourselves

in the charred mirrors
and ponds of rainwater.
My ears, picking my name out

of the wind howling between
tarp and roof, are as presumptuous as ever.
This is how my feet get involved

in the business
of finding a laminate dance floor
beneath debris—involved in wanting more.

My father might've followed a woman
onto a floor like this
and there had to have been

a shotgun of light from the disco ball
and a crowd disappearing.
That happened once, right?

yas ⎡ My memory is a liar.
⎬ Claims to know what it can't.
⎣ But still, I let it narrate

the time when rooms like this
were more than rooms like this.
Even if I know nothing of walls

beyond their tendency to lean
and give up. One can only hold so much
without having to give it all away.

# Megalophobia
*Fear of large things*

It's not that the walls are closing in. I mean,
look at his shoulders. They widen even as we speak.
That blazer is tearing on the blades,
and nothing's ever going to fit again. He's not afraid
the falling ceiling will flatten him to the floor,
it's the way those shins add inches, the way
they propel him upward. He doesn't look comfortable
being so sky-bound. The tight spaces kept him
vibrating to himself and now here they come,
asking the boy to be bigger than the room will allow,
to breathe the way a hurricane breathes.

When they say, *C'mon, be a man*, don't they hear
the barbells hitting the floor in his head? Don't you
hear the way furniture scrapes and appliances rattle
like the whole rabble either wants to escape
or wants to warn us
that when giants are needled out of slumber
they make a mess of neatly arranged mountains?

As if we don't know how to be anything
but an elbow cracking the Earth in half.

# Intake in the Ward

Said he never saw that shit coming. A knot
rose like a knuckle out of his hair. The guitarist
told me he lost his fender to the sea
of sweaty elbows when he unplugged it
and dove into the mosh pit.

After the intake he admitted he really sold the strat
and amp and stomp boxes for booze and food,
ate alone, pushed away from the plate,
with its tongue-shaped ketchup smears,
and went directly to an orgy. Said his grief

needed a stage that fit:
a soundtrack of strangers fucking
and forgetting. *It's easier than you think
to get invited to one.*
When I told him I didn't need to know this

for the intake, he rolled up his shirt,
exposed the bruise-smeared surface,
and asked if I needed to know which he took,
which were given, which were paid for,
and what defects had cost him the most.

# The Hollow Made by Her Open Fist

The first time a woman said *choke me*,
though I cringed at how well her breath-full
stalk fit into the hollow made by my open fist

and marveled at how much pressure
I could apply without actually stopping
her exhalation and whispered instructions,

I still never hesitated.
Not even as I cringed
at how easily it conjured

the perfection with which
the larger man's forearm fit
under my chin, as he pointed a gun

so small
I thought it was a toy
until he cocked it and whispered,

*I'll fucking kill you.*
There should be a Freudian
version of this encounter where,

pinned by this man, my erection
rises at the same slow pace of a pistol
pressing deeper into the salt of my cheek.

But if I was just a flaccid boy then,
wriggling like a fly whose motion
only calls forth an eight-legged death,

am I more accountable for the tingle
she loves to feel skitter across scalp
after the hair has been pulled taut like a web?

The first time I told a woman
to choke me, I never actually told her
to choke me, but what became clear

when my cheek burned against her rug, jaw
turned to one side under her filament-soft palm
was the echo we'd stifle if my throat didn't yield.

# It Shakes Us Still

After the Baptist retreat cartoons
and health class slide show insisted
sex was only good for courting AIDS
and babies and pustules, a fingernail
traced across chest earthquakes us still,
and the gods still build hearts
like hearths in homeless shelters,
a permanent place for the temporary
to gather and liquefy the frost on their hands.
An ungloved hand in winter slid under shirt
still shakes the ice free. No one believes me
when I say his ten fingers, together,
are the smallest cult or choir gathered
to worship the smallest demon or deity
except for the pastor. This makes sense to him
the way animation always will to me,
even at an age when time has hurled
all its hand grenades at the imagination.
And because this is where I learned
the incorrect color of hearts

and that giving a hug means taking one back,
I'll always believe the bodily destruction
that waits at the bottom of a gorge
for those of us stupid enough to look down
isn't stupid enough to try to kill
the coyote in our blood that made us leap.

# The Whetting of Teeth

Tomorrow wears a smile that nobody can use,
mocks the way I spend this now: keystrokes and wine,
sex and the desire for sex. He demands we lose
ourselves, stare in the mirror of his face sometimes,
question what we do in the light of computer
screens and in the tangles of sheets to deserve him.
Can't we see he's wearing his best smirk? Look closer
at us—at me, dressed in what I always dress in:

skin and skin. Even I'm tired of dragging this
outfit in front of my mirror. So, imagine
what Tomorrow thinks. If he asked, *What have you missed
today?* I couldn't respond honestly, *This wine,
her voice, some word, a particular scent,*
without feeling silly, or at least, redundant.

Without feeling silly or even redundant,
I say, *I love the body* and *I love the word*.
Notice the similarity to hymn or chant.

I think of my dad's church, me being handed the lord,
wondering why someone decides to be a word,

and if this man offered his blood and flesh, what had
we become now that we were all lined up like words

in scriptures, arranged neatly on pews like suit-clad
lines of verse consuming a man before we pray?
Why are dreams the only place these answers feel close?

When you woke me at my desk, you kissed wine away
from the corners of my lips, and went on to note

that it looked like blood in dim light, mocking again,
*Who's been devoured now, my lovely, vicious man?*

Who've you devoured now, lovely-vicious man?
She called to ask for the trinkets you pilfered.
Give this woman what is owed: shiraz or spit, strands
of hair, unopened letters, or just blank paper
where this word or psalm was supposed to go. The space
you left open inside a dry ring of wine, what
can fill that? It will never fit around my waist.
We'll never fit inside your mouth. Despite how much
you beg for communion, try and kiss the hips holy,
my size can't be altered by a prayer or a wish.
Trust me. Her clothes won't make you any less lonely.
I know the consumed; they want to consume, and this
want is saltwater that keeps spilling over
into our mouths when we praise each other.

Inside our mouths, when we praise each other,
there are never wafers.                    We hold the taste

of lovers on our tongues and bite down. *Bite
me,* she insisted, breathless—you nibbled
the shoulder.                    Because she has never known

restraint, those starved fingers will pierce and hold
until that moment is eternity,
since the next woman you hold will always
ask where nicks and scars come from.          If it hurt.

Tell her the truth.          She will demand a place
on your back that stirs wonder in women
too, a place where questions lead back to her

lunular cuts, half question marks, and her
skin is a barrier broken between teeth.

Skin becomes a barrier broken between teeth.
When what is under the surface thrashes in praise,
blood becomes a prisoner pardoned and released
from our shuttered facilities. Have we always
made such charming prisons, full of so many cells?
Tomorrow says that we are either asylums
or we are their inmates, but we can't always tell
which side of the wall we die on, what we die from,
or who's doing the killing, even as blood splashes
like flames against the hospital that is an island
that is sinking in heat. Yes, it will be ashes
tomorrow, but we can't fight off the call to stand
in its shrinking halls. I scour these rooms where air
closes like fists on the handrims of a wheel chair.

Closed fists on the handrims of his wheelchair.
Screams when orderlies approach his window
to drag him away. It's time to prepare
for flailing, the refusal to swallow
peas. He claims the rooms are controlling him.

That's on a good day; others he scratches,
bites, or throws himself down on linoleum,
goes limp and sobs as he's lifted like a sack.

Have you ever been to a room like this,
where you hate the corners and start to loathe
dust? Maybe sanctuaries make you wish
you could stop the walls that collapse and close
in until there's barely enough room left over
to sweat, as if clenched in the arms of a lover.

Sweat as if clenched in the arms of a lover.
Bleed as if you are tangled in barbed wire. Take
whatever fits into your mouth: fervor
and need, grapes and skin—hold them and make
sure those points sink deep, because fingertips
are flimsy at holding what we can't own.
I need your teeth in me, slow and vicious,
to tell me my armor is just skin, bones,
only bones. I shouldn't have laughed when you
told me you'd pray for me until blood rolled
like wine. Forgive me; by then I was too
drunk—too sober, maybe—I only know
that, like you, I will have a mouth full of sharp tools
tomorrow. Smiles. But nothing our bodies can use.

# Sugar

Talk to him any day of the week and it's all black. Talk
of the cost of insulin. The bitch he married. It's all
snuffed-up spit staining a paper cup. The hand.
The blanket across knees.

Talk to the home nurse. It's all stringy hands
clutching at a skirt, the soft give of poplin,
and her new nickname: *Juicy*.
The chair and its wheels
*that ain't goin' no-goddamn-where*. A trap. Damn legs;

they kicked a bitch in her distended stomach once.
Trying to kill the puppies—killed the bitch.
Found him this way: A dry cleaning bag duct-taped
around his own fool head
with air holes pierced under the nose. Found him

at the edge of the driveway *heading back to Stockton*.
Blood sugar through the stucco ceiling.
The cost of insulin pissing him off.
His daughter pays for the insulin. Found him this way:
Cursing out the quiet girl

on the lawn. She won't move
because she's made of fired clay.
A terracotta statue. *I'll get you back for this?*
All the talk is blood-black gauze
where a toe was. *You did this to me, Juicy.*

Found him limp on the porch.
Calling out in his sleep for the bitch
he married. Some folks still call diabetes *the sugar*. The woman
he calls out to, been dead from it for years.

# Death Scene in a Psychiatric Ward

*What's my motivation?*


You're a human,
and they've taken everything from you:
shoes, belt, copper bracelet,
lighter, and rosary.
You're empty—
your stomach withers against your ribs
because you refuse to eat
without a lawyer present.
You're not under arrest,
not on trial—just here,
with these claw marks on the walls
in The Quiet Room and scraping every night.
Millipedes are everywhere. Legs are hundreds
of eyelashes blinking just over the skin
and just under the skin
but don't worry about them;
no one can see the bugs
except you, and you
pretend not to because you're hoping
for an early release. Don't react.
You can feel them
skitter but don't react.
You don't want to slam your head

against cinder block until it splits.
You *need* to because you can hear
the gears turning in the walls
and you know they're inching closer.
This grease-blotched tile is where you lie
and face the ceiling in a trance.
Vishnu will enter the room surrounded
by light, but don't look for that;
a computer will fabricate the image in post
like that scene where a giant statue of Buddha
crashes down a waterfall.

Ok, so we'll start with the top-down shot.
Remember, you're scared.
You're alone. You don't trust your senses,
and we're gonna' need two takes:
one with your eyes closed
and the other.

# Behind the Ward

are handfuls of confused hair
in a dust mop
with a broken handle.

gauze still wet
from the business of the day:
the outburst,
vomit-pink stains
from an attempted escape—
blood breaking out of the wrists.

mildewed boxes hold
decks of playing cards
cut into sevenths
and reassembled with tape.

there are letters.

this one:

>To a paper crane,
>I've got the wind you want…

this one:

>To fingernails,

Come home soon…

this one:

      To a trucker still en route,
      When you asked what I did,
      I said I slammed my head in the van door
      and passed out in the driveway
      because I wanted you

      to leave me alone.

      Hope this never finds you.

# Ode to Forgetting

I know how to lie still when wind
makes grass writhe against me like snakes.

I want the snakes to carry me away.
I've always been too big for this,

even before my first kiss
trapped me against a garage,

its peeling paint scratching new
patterns into my back.

I tried to read lines on skin.
Looked for maps out of myself.

I've wanted to get carried away
for years. Not even the gale

that foreshadowed the storm
that tore a tree out of ground

can come close to lifting me.
Too much in my pockets I suppose:

an assortment of keys to locks
that have long been forgotten.

Maybe forgotten isn't the same
as lost, and lost isn't the same

as dead. I forget dead folks all the time.
The space they used to take up is filling

with something like air but breathable.
Just the other night, a silhouette arrived

clothed in a moment I couldn't recall.
Even cities I've seen and seen are naked and new,

a coterie of streets named I Thought I Knew the Way
and Her House Used To Be Somewhere Near Here.

# Better Devices

A better gizmo than him would know
how to find the line of locks
trailing from arm pit to waist, unfasten each,
and expose the leaf-shaped beacon,
so that its iambic pulse of light
could lead the search party to the woods
he finds himself lost in again.

A better device wouldn't get lost
among the trees to begin with.
Good devices don't wander off. They go on
peeling the lid off this and fusing rivets to that
without thinking much
about the way pine stirs the sensors
and confuses memory enough to transform

wandering into a function that is necessary
for the maintenance of that vessel
full of ionized ball bearings in his head.

# God of the Ocean of Lumber

The air in this world is thicker than I remember
from nights at camp, whacking fireflies
with a fallen branch, wondering if the shadows
that numbered in the hundreds
were all cast by the same god
I hung out with when I was little—his voice
is the silence I've been afraid of hearing ever since.
I used to smack the side of a tree
until the rust-red leaves showered me
and I felt stronger than god;
I could've cracked his moon in half
if I wanted to—if I swung my stick high
and hard enough, if I screamed
loud enough. But I'm afraid to know what happens
when *enough* is the sound of my staff splintering
against heaven,
a shock up my arm—
                            No gods, still,
even after I broke away
from the campfire and its songs so I could kneel
in the woods and let wild grass grow
around my damp knees. To kneel with a question and rise
with a question is only one way to forget
your old prayers. Another is to busy your hands

with sticks, carving your runes into a clearing's mud.
I learned dead trees could be toppled
by small hands if the rot was deep enough
and there was plenty of leverage.
They creaked, cracked, and tumbled
down to—
                    I don't know where;
my eyes couldn't follow that far in the dark.
I like to think there was another camp at the bottom,
where they worshiped a god of wood and sap, and nightly,
when I snuck from my tent, I responded to their prayers
with a sign: this very wood
crashing down around them.

# Water Devil

Spout of a leaf,
listen out for the screams
of your relentless audience:
the applause of a waterfall
in the distance,

a hurricane looting
a Miami shopping mall.
How careful you are
with the rain-cradling
curve of your back.

Near your forest,
all are ready to swim
and happy to drown
in me: this lake of fire
that moats the edge.

From my mouth,
they come to peel the flames
and drink their slick throats
into the most silent ash.

# Little Design
*After Li-Young Lee*

I painted my lover
on a lake.
Since then, the fish
bathe her every morning
and slide slippers on her
feet every night.

I painted my lover on a glacier.
Since then, my gloves
are always on,
and all the snow
has become a gallery
whose exhibits are the evenings,
whose plinths
stand unwavering. Sometimes
I tip them over
on purpose
for a chance to exhume the shards.

I painted my lover
under my sternum.

Now she courses through me,
strange ink, little calligraphy
stroke, brilliant well of pitch-black.

A vast constellation-free night
to dip the quill of a tongue into.

# The Spirit Names of Stolen Books

Every one of your books I told you went missing,
I kept, rain-ruined, wrapped in your denim jacket

on the backseat of my Fusion for so many months
they carry new names like the passing months;

I call your copy of *Song*, *Ruby-Mouth*, and last night
I sat in the lamplight with *Clean-Tooth*,

whom you know as *Ariel*, and *the smile of the snow*
she mentions was nearly toothless by then,

the rain having come early to punch (w)holes in it.
I change(d) into a white bat for winter — invisible

in a blizzard and conspicuous on a clear night.
My leucistic fur ripples as I dive into a chimney.

I won't be long here—good thief that I am. Quiet
like soot gathering. Quiet like failing embers.

Quiet trees send their shadows to keep me company
on the walk home; my wings are too noisy for flight.

Their leathery snap might startle flurries
only just now returning to their sleepy ways.

Too awake they were when I left the city.
They gathered for warmth in the grill of my car

as I eked out the miles until the gathering
distance meant there was no way to give back

what a cascade of spring storms had broken
all the rules of heaven to come here and claim.

# History as Road Trip from Detroit to Mississippi

Coming black * I read "back"
into the deep south,
my friend says,
is like returning
to an elegant home
you were beaten in
as a child.
I press my head to glass
and try to interpret
the landscape
turning dark as the sun
surrenders again.

This drive is an inhale
needing exhale
but terrified of it.
To breathe out
is to let go
and letting go
might be a pastime
best left to historians.

Here's the whole hollow
of a dog's chest

on the road rising
like an artifact. Fossil. Here
is the heat hanging low
enough to make mirage.
Here is the puddle
no one can drink from.

Here in this land
or whatever it is
the gods used
to call land,
I become more us
than me, more
blistered sole
and sore

and dogwood
and all of us
and all of this
looking back

into the agrarian
cage made of
all these rising
stems, from blood

to whatever it is
the gods used
to call blood,
and see my limbs
for what they are:
kindling.
It's what context does—

the mouth that keeps
opening wider
to take in the memory,
gnaw until it is mangled
and disfigured

like history,
and what else
could we ask of history
but to mimic

whatever is chewed
and spit
at our constantly
re-arriving feet?

# To Detroiters I Too May Have Called by the Wrong Names

Sorry. When I called you a graveyard,
I meant your round, stone teeth
always make me laugh.
When I said you couldn't touch me,
I meant, tag you're it. Follow me! Follow me!
I called you a tangle of vines because
you didn't let me fall
out of love with your hair.

When I called you a land of too much sleep,
I meant keep dreaming me up
and I'll keep dreaming of you.
And since I can't be anything but a mirror
facing another mirror when I walk past a building,
I have to stare into us rudely. You're nosey
like me, and curious like me,
so you know I have to wander some
and wonder more
which holes need to be patched
and which are here to offer another view.

I never meant to curse you with my dead,
but since they'll come for you anyway,
family, may every ghost find you

ready to wrestle them into canvas or wood.
May every haunting be a symphony
of wind through every hollow
and every tree, and every corner
of every structure be a violin's bridge
you cross or burn, breathing like a vibrated note.

Sisters and brothers of the vibrato,
of the backyard smoke, of the Nain Rouge,
I know your kind of red, roja,
how it blends impossibly with blue,
how it smears the bruise of you
to color an evening into the next sunrise purple.
Mirror, last night you slept
and I became a camera in front of your film.
Then a finger stepped on a guitar string
and an endless workday fell away
just like that. A paintbrush spoke plainly to a hand.
A mural crept up a wall without waking anyone,
and a microphone trapped the sound of a siren
on a bedroom mixtape forever.

Detroit, when I said you're dreaming, I meant,
you *are* dreaming. Keep making me up.
When I said your pet phoenix was a bad omen,
I should've said, I read way too many comic books

and I just wish it could breathe fire.
I told you my back itches where the wings used to be,
but I meant, will anyone still believe me
when I whisper my song about flight?

What I meant by, let the trappers come,
was when they do, let them
bring their most gilded cages
that they might know there are birds
yes, but also, here
there be dragons—mad dragons, son.
May your forked tongues
always be surrounded by fire.
Your wings a deafening applause.
I've written your feathers across me,
and now I marvel at your scales.
May I always be infinitesimal and infinite
in your belly. Swallow my whole heart whole.

And when they come to defang you, Beast,
Brother, Love, Sister, Art, City,
may they find the streets jagged
with the previous conquerors' teeth.

# Exit Interview

What do I know of the width of your chest?
The muscle that keeps the heart at bay?
What of ink-needled shoulder blades?
How much metal in the taste of blood
on your bitten tongue? How many wreaths,
casts, gauze-covered stumps, and wired jaws?
What do I know of the heavy gurneys?
What don't I know about the road
that leads to anywhere but where you stand
becoming the most winding and most covered
in shards of disappointing days?
What is there to say to you
when you return with the same eyes
that clench compulsively like beetles
always under assault, if not that I have missed
the fucked-up way you're always going to be
when there's a chance to take off your shirt,
skin flush with a scream that will almost be heard?

# In the Future You Will Be Your Own Therapist

Even if they program the thing to sound like you
and furrow its brow the way you do when you wince
and they match your brain synapse for synapse, timing
every fire so that it blinks when you blink and hates
the same music that makes your teeth itch,
won't it still make a pretty shitty therapist?

Say they send the thing to a better middle school than yours
where no one shoves it into anything and it develops
the confidence to kiss the girl or boy that would have made you
piss yourself if they ever came close, and this thing
gets programmed to not get caught
jacking off and makes it through undergrad,
and they arrange to have you sit on a couch
in this thing's office—will it ever have anything to say
about the funerals it missed?

Won't the fingers that want nothing to do with the tie
they fumble into uneven lines
look disappointingly like the fingers
that fumble the pen? Drop the notebook?

# Your Life Prepared You for a Career in Film

*How's our hero going to get out of this one?*

Yes, the narrator in your head is cliché.
And so is the director, with his Dutch angles
and blinding smoke machine.
Wardrobe stuffs you in the same wrinkled suit
you've been trying to take off
since you were old enough to handle its buttons.


The script you wrote calls for a happy ending
but a note from the boardroom demands
what is described only as a
*Good.*
*Slow.*
*Death.*


Twenty lines of dialogue describe death as
*the six beneath forever,*
*the eternal high five,*
*God's after party,*
*spooning with Satan,*
and of course,
*meeting the great bible salesman in the sky.*

*Six gods, Satan and a Bible salesman walk into a bar,*
begins one scene in which
the word "escape" is defined as a broken glass
to try and drink from without getting cut.

So face it, you'll always end up
on the cutting room floor.
There's always going to be just one more heist,
and you'll always be too old for this shit.
You've got a short fuse, you don't play by the rules,
you drink like a gutter, and you sure as hell
don't need a partner. We get it—
you work alone. But this
is the score of a lifetime or
the last chance for a cure or
the case of a lifetime or
the only way to make sure
your family is safe in the final act,
and you are never too old for this.

I know locker after locker is stuffed with you,
your glasses are tapped and re-tapped,
your skin is a minefield,
but your life prepared you for a career in film;
you can hack a Norad satellite with a pocket calculator,
the magic was you all along,
and the strange kid you're afraid to admit

you want to get strange with
knows the ancient rom-com secret
of lifting glasses.

Yes, you will be shot,
but only in your off arm.
You'll still wield a pistol like the lightning of Zeus,
arrive just in time, lean in for the kiss
only to be interrupted by an explosion,
or questions from small children
or the one guard you forgot to knock out. Yes,
you will be riddled with bullets.
But saved by the Bible in your left breast pocket.
Yes, you will be shot
one day from retirement and die
in the arms of a better looking character.
And yes it will be too soon.

You once watched someone close to you
leave a room like smoke
and soon you'll watch someone close to the room
leave and return as a ghost.
She'll have all the answers
but only offer more questions

like, *Are you just going to pretend forever, Jamaal?*

Please never stop.
The guy who plays you in the sequel
can't make an entrance like you,
the light bulbs go cold and frost surrounds
the entrance of you.
I never thought you'd escape the moving walls
but you did, and when you did
I was mad, rabid,
and cheering for you.

# Parallel Existence

My friend wònders why she has to be
*one of those motherfuckers with two of everything.*
Why that backup tin of sewing needles?
Why two packs of cotton balls?
She admits to owning multiple packs of razor
multipacks in case she has to change
the bathroom decor.
*Both are open. It's a problem.*

She's packing it all up tonight, these knickknacks
from some parallel life she knows nothing about,
except that her decisions in that one
must be more cherry tree planted in the yard
and less painful kisses in the back room
of a sandwich shop.

I think maybe we need more spools of thread,
suture kits, and staples set aside in case
we have to retreat to one of those other dimensions
that, with every new choice, split and sprawl

like paths across a struck windshield. *No, Jamaal,*
she says, *you don't understand.*

*I have to get rid of it. This shit is piling up.*

# Dare

A woman presses a thumb
into the eye socket
of a dead doe, recoils,
then sticks in her pinky.
Dare doesn't mean the same thing
when you dare yourself, does it?
A dare is something like a gift—sure
you can give it to yourself
but when you tear the metallic paper,
it's good to have someone there
to show the broken thing to.
Of course it's broken.
They dared me to throw it from a balcony
before opening it. They dared me to break
into a liquor store and why not?
It was the summer of 2003,
and the North Atlantic power grid was down.
I stuck my finger in a socket to prove it.
When no specter of current leapt out,
eager to scale the stupid architecture of me
and blacken its wiring, I thought,
*Why not?* and stuck it in again.

# Shift

Acting on an anonymous tip, my shift supervisor
at a runaway shelter strip-searched six teenagers.
My first-grade teacher was taping shut the mouths
of talkative students by the time she neared retirement,
and Mr. Vickers, a skilled electrician in his day,
didn't adapt when fuse boxes became circuit breakers,
a fact that didn't stop him from tinkering
in our basement until the house was consumed by flame.

I used to want to be this bad at a job.
I wanted to show up pissy drunk to staff meetings
when the powerpoint slides were already dissolving
one into another, but I had this bad habit
of showing up on time and more sober
than any man should be when working
audio/visual hospitality in a three-star hotel
that was a four-star hotel
before he started working there.

When the entire North Atlantic blacked out,
every soul in the Hyatt Regency Dearborn flooded
the parking lot panicked about terrorists and rapture,
while I plugged in microphones and taped down cables
by flashlight—you know, in case whatever cataclysm

102

that was unfolding didn't preempt the meetings.
Meetings, before which, I was told to convince
a children's hospital to pay fifteen dollars
to rent a nine-dollar laser pointer. Good job,
the big pharm rep said, while passing me
a hefty tip that made me wonder: is it good
to be good at a job if that job involves pretending
to be a secret service agent for a George Bush
impersonator hired by Pfizer? I don't know

if it's better to be good at a bad job or bad at a good job,
but there must be some kind of satisfaction
in doing a job so poorly, you are never asked to do it again.
I'm not saying he's a hero, but there's a guy out there
who overloaded a transformer and made a difference,
because in a moment, sweating through my suit,
groping in the dark when my boss was safe at home,

I learned that I'd work any job this hard, ache
like this to know that I could always ache for something.
There's a hell for people like us
where we shovel the coal we have mined ourselves
into furnaces that burn the flesh from our bones
nightly, and we never miss a shift.

# Bad Day

To be honest, the day did fine.
I'm the one who donated the tip of my thumb
to chopped onion and cilantro.

The room filling with the scent
of singed hair from where the iron kissed my thigh
is another creation all my own.

The day did its best to fill every
inbox with not so terrible news, and then fill
my memory with redolence.

The day even turned down
the train's volume, turned up the sun, hid the pills,
used my elbow to empty

a bottle of bourbon in the car,
and managed, somehow, to keep them all—
every person I love — alive

for another twenty-four hours,
the constant call from inside the grave-mouth
barely a murmer for now.

# For Years You Trained for Being Lost at Sea

With the spyglass extended,
lean all the way out.
Worry not how your ship
will stay afloat if your ship

is a tire or box
because these are not waves.
This is a grassless backyard.
The system of canals underneath

were tunneled by earthworms
that will come to greet you
next rainfall. Worry not
how they breathe.

Focus on the island glinting
just out of reach and mark
the similarity *barely too far*
holds to *close enough*
*to have to try.*

# Unsigned Letter to a Human in the 21st Century

Dear citizen of the binary mirror,
Dear wide-eyed and deft-fingered,
Dear deer in an ex-forest clearing,

Please forgive me if I'm speaking too soon.
Are you here yet?
Or is it that your presence only looks like arrival
because you can't help but be the loudest ghost?
If that wasn't you I saw
moving toward the edge of a cliff
like a moth to a moth
that flutters in flames,
no worries. I'll leave this here for another time.

I write you because you asked me to,
though you may not remember the call,
though we may not have ever spoken.
But I heard it in your verse
after you bit your tongue
and bragged about the blood.
Dear aspirant to the throne
of Most Unassailable Victim,

I write you because when I opened my mouth

to say *love,* someone said sword again.
But Rumi said *love,*
and so I'm out in New England again
and in Detroit again
and in America still
with my ear pressed to this red book
and sure enough, the harsh sound
of a scabbard emptying
so that a belly could fill with blade
was drowned out for a moment,
as Love went running down the mountainside
out into the everything, becoming
the mad man again.
I closed my eyes and opened
what I didn't know was locked inside,
and even now, I fumble for its name.
Could it have been the opening itself?


I write to confess I've known for years
that the closed-off parts of me
need the closed-off parts of you.
You are full of more you than is known,
and I confess I never bothered to notice.
But now I notice everything.
How my sink holds a sea,
overflows and becomes a
waterfall, becomes a puddle

at my feet. There's an ancient article
from just seven years ago on waterboarding.
Another provides a litany
of the best ways to be ok with everything
our hearts stutter about: the bleach-white coral,
the pistol-full avenues,
the lucrative penitentiaries,
and women's shelters that bulge with bruise.
They say the starved are guilty
of being hungry, and the head-scarfed girl
is guilty of living near the detonation,
and now I notice my hands—
how little they hold. They are teacups
bailing out this vessel
not worthy of any sea, and silence
is the rag stuffed into the mouth
of a gurgling drain. But I digress.

Dear digital city,

Scrolling around our world's web
I opened another window
full of the seething news.
But this time, I could only laugh
at what Destruction had cloaked itself in.

If the gauze-like veil had a name, it would be
something along the lines of *Inevitability*.
But you are training in an alchemy
that can make those first three syllables fall away.
Destruction doesn't know the strike
in the middle of it is past tense;
let the shark spin in its cage.
We only need to live long enough to teach
those who will, tomorrow,
drown it in the air.


My friend,


I write because I love you enough
to ask for what is terrible: run farther
than your feet can possibly carry your heart.
I love you enough to confess that you will fail
but fail closer to the finish line
than if you lie down when the start gun fires.
And in this way, you will never fail
to be arch, stepping-stone, bridge
of bone and intellect,
of guts and song. Look
how lively the children step.

Let's nod our heads to their footfalls.
Become backbeat with me
and they will sing the harmonics
we forgot to learn.

Tell me you wouldn't die for that.

Tell me you will live for this.

Love,

# Letter to Matthew Olzmann
# Regarding Sirens and Shipwrecks

Dear Matt,

I keep telling myself the boat wasn't so bad,
but its silence still spreads. It still spills
out of that story in which you write letter after letter
to the L.R. Doty, though the ship's voice
just reverberates with the hollow timbre
of any submerged god. So, yeah, fam.
Fuck that boat.


Thank you for your last missive
and the unicorn horn folded inside.
I'm not brave enough to taste
the pale powder yet, but I'm honored
by the wizardry of your letter.
Of all the letters I've written, the most useless
were scribbled by my voice at the foot of a bed.
I uttered enough unfulfilled requests
that I stopped being afraid of the villains
I scribbled into comic book panels.
Turns out the ocean-god
that invaded from another dimension
was trapped in the wood of my sketch pencil all along.
Have you considered world domination?
This isn't to say you'd succeed,

or even that you'd be good at it if you did.
Just that you'd look damn good doing it,
and I'd always back you up on doomsday laser.

Speaking of looking good,
I've met a woman who assures me
my course is right, despite the choppiness
of waves. In the Radiohead song,
*there's always a siren singing you to shipwreck,*
but I can tell her music is lighthouse.
And you should see the way she commands water,
shaping it with her fingertips,
folding it into corners small enough to swallow.
A shipwright assured me
boats can't be built out of ocean anymore
than an ocean can be made of lumber,
but when I pointed to a forest...

# This is How I Know It Might Work
*After Matthew Olzmann, for Tarfia*

Because your head is a rec room
full of the best toys,
and your second skull is a crate
full of the greatest records
anyone can be ashamed of.
Because you give good whiskey and bacon
no quarter. Because I want to be sober
the next time I hold you
and because that is new. As is the need
for roses with no mention of blood,
and because I always mentioned blood,
whenever someone mentioned roses,
and you taught me it was ok
to grab them all by the stem.


Because you cross the roses out of my poems.
Because you sang me a song
that made no sense and didn't pretend it did.
Because you insert roses into my poems
and play an instrument I've only heard
through a laptop speaker when you were oceans
too far. Because you are generous.
Because you are greedy. Because you grab
at all of the voices you can lift,

even the broken ones—
especially the broken ones—
and bury them under your hair
until compositions grow.

Because I want to remove the rain cloud over your head—
I mean—I want to replace the rain cloud
over your head; become your private storm.
I like the way you carry a storm.
Carry me. I'll downpour for you
and run my fingers through the language
that sprouts like a garden of paper flowers
you make erupt perennial
when the page is an empty field
and not even stillness will do.

# Against Against

Someone said love should never appear
in a poem and I wondered
what to do if I love

the cicatrix of a leaf the way I love
the pattern of nerves fanning out
on an anatomy poster

or the divergent and converging
futures trailing across
our palms.

When they said to remove the modifiers
I wasn't sure what one should say
if the morgues of their cities

truly are ravenous and the darkness
has always been hunger-full.
And speaking of darkness—

And speaking of weariness and failure
and iniquity and silence and enmity—
why not abstract?

Why not detachment from the weight
of driftwood, mercurial fish,
seaweed, mermaid,

sea serpent—whatever objects the nets
are hauled in heavy with
this week

of empty shoreline—this week
of waking up still
missing?

# And for My Last Trick

I'll slice the onions so thin
they disintegrate against cast-iron black.
No one likes this trick
as much as the hoop of fire
I used to jump through, but at least
I don't get the shakes anymore. The burning
gasoline smelled like the empty living room
of our home going up.
It was ridiculous of me to think
anyone would see this
as a metaphor for entering
and exiting the center of a life
that's always going up in flames.
Existence is what I mean.
I enter the loop. I exit the loop.
Not touching the sides
is my only accomplishment,
but still, the gateway burns
and the doorway shrinks,
so I had quit that ruse.

The sizzling skillet, round and full
of what I've cried over to cut
is not metaphor for anything.
It is only delicious.
As all leaving things are.

"I come from a country where you have to
rebuild your house every day."
—Luljeta Lleshanaku

# Book Benefactors

Alice James Books wishes to thank the following individuals who generously contributed toward the publication of The Big Book of Exit Strategies:

Risa Denenberg
Ellen Doré Watson
Thomas Whayne

For more information about AJB's book benefactor program, contact us via phone or email, or visit alicejamesbooks.org to see a list of forthcoming titles.

# Recent Titles from Alice James Books

*play dead*, francine j. harris

*Thief in the Interior,* Phillip B. Williams

*Second Empire,* Richie Hofmann

*Drought-Adapted Vine*, Donald Revell

*Refuge/es,* Michael Broek

*O'Nights,* Cecily Parks

*Yearling*, Lo Kwa Mei-en

*Sand Opera*, Philip Metres

*Devil, Dear,* Mary Ann McFadden

*Eros Is More*, Juan Antonio González Iglesias,
Translated by Curtis Bauer

*Mad Honey Symposium,* Sally Wen Mao

*Split,* Cathy Linh Che

*Money Money Money | Water Water Water,* Jane Mead

*Orphan,* Jan Heller Levi

*Hum,* Jamaal May

*Viral*, Suzanne Parker

*We Come Elemental*, Tamiko Beyer

*Obscenely Yours*, Angelo Nikolopoulos

*Mezzanines*, Matthew Olzmann

*Lit from Inside: 40 Years of Poetry from Alice James Books*,
Edited by Anne Marie Macari and Carey Salerno

*Black Crow Dress*, Roxane Beth Johnson

*Dark Elderberry Branch: Poems of Marina Tsvetaeva*,
A Reading by Ilya Kaminsky and Jean Valentine

*Tantivy*, Donald Revell

*Murder Ballad*, Jane Springer

Alice James Books has been publishing poetry since 1973. The press was founded in Boston, Massachusetts as a cooperative wherein authors performed the day-to-day undertakings of the press. This collaborative element remains viable even today, as authors who publish with the press are also invited to become members of the editorial board and participate in editorial decisions at the press. The editorial board selects manuscripts for publication via the press's annual, national competition, the Alice James Award. Alice James Books seeks to support women writers and was named for Alice James, sister to William and Henry, whose extraordinary gift for writing went unrecognized during her lifetime.


Designed by Pamela A. Consolazio
LITTLE FROG DESIGNS

Printed by McNaughton & Gunn